30 DAYS TO START AND GROW YOUR OWN CPR AND SAFETY TRAINING BUSINESS

A STEP-BY-STEP GUIDE TO LAUNCH, ATTRACT CLIENTS & MAKE A PROFIT

By

TIMEKA MAPP

Copyright © 2013, 2026

WHAT IS A CPR AND SAFETY TRAINING BUSINESS?

At its core, a CPR and Safety Training business is a **life-saving enterprise**. You provide the bridge between a medical emergency and the arrival of professional first responders. By offering specialized training in Cardiopulmonary Resuscitation (CPR), Automated External Defibrillator (AED) use, and Basic First Aid, you empower everyday citizens and professionals alike to act when seconds count.

Beyond the Classroom: A Multi-Stream Revenue Model

In today's market, a successful safety business is more than just a lecture in a rented room. It is a comprehensive safety solution that includes:

- **Certified Training:** Authorized courses through the **American Heart Association (AHA)**, **Red Cross**, or **Health & Safety Institute (HSI)**.
- **Blended Learning:** A modern "Phygital" approach combining online theory with rapid, in-person hands-on skills assessments.

- **Corporate Compliance:** Helping businesses meet **OSHA** requirements through scheduled staff certifications and risk assessments.
- **Safety Consulting:** Providing site inspections, emergency response planning, and AED program management.

The Mission

The goal of this business is to build a "Nation of Lifesavers." You are providing more than a certificate; you are providing the **authority to act**. Whether your clients are healthcare professionals needing BLS (Basic Life Support) credentials or new parents wanting peace of mind, your business ensures that when a heartbeat stops, your students have the skills to start it again.

How To Use This Book

This book serves as your professional roadmap, providing the specialized knowledge and strategic skills necessary to launch a thriving CPR and safety training business. Every chapter is a building block, carefully outlining the path from initial research to advanced financial management. With these pages as your foundation, you can move forward with the absolute confidence that you are building on a proven model.

Your Path to a Scalable System

The primary objective of this guide is to provide you with a streamlined, successful system for modern business ownership. We recognize that while certifications are the baseline, a **truly successful** business is built on clarity of purpose and efficient operations. By following this guide, you are ensuring that every aspect of your business—from marketing to team building—is grounded in excellence.

Strategies for Success

To maximize your results, approach each day as a new milestone. We have designed this journey to be:

- **Comprehensive:** Covering everything from local licensing to high-level government contracting.
- **Actionable:** Providing clear steps so you can see tangible progress every single day.
- **Systems-Oriented:** Focused on creating a business that is organized, professional, and ready to scale.

By utilizing the information in this book, you are laying the groundwork for a business that not only meets industry standards but sets new ones. You are now equipped to turn your passion for safety into a profitable and impactful reality.

Let's Get Started

By opening this book, today becomes the official Day One of your journey to creating a spectacular CPR and safety training business. You are choosing to invest your time, your energy, and your vision into a venture that truly matters. This commitment to your future and your community is a significant milestone, and it is absolutely worth celebrating!

As a coach, I feel immense excitement whenever I begin working with a new client. There is a unique joy in learning about your specific goals, the audience you are called to serve, and the story you want to tell through your brand. It is a profound honor to be trusted with your vision. One of the most rewarding parts of my work is seeing the transformation in my **Seven Figure CPR and Safety Training Business Academy** clients as they realize exactly what we can achieve together.

Your Path to Implementation

To achieve the highest level of success, I invite you to commit to this process fully. The most effective way to build momentum is to pair your learning with immediate action. You have everything you need to succeed right here.

- **Be Decisive:** Trust your intuition and the proven steps laid out for you.
- **Be Proactive:** Jump directly into the tasks and watch your business take shape.
- **Be a Creator:** Move beyond consuming information and become an active builder of your brand.

You are here to make a difference and build a profitable legacy. Let's dive in and start creating your success story today!

TABLE OF CONTENTS

Legal Notes

Day 1: Research The Market & Identify Your CPR And Safety Training Target Audience

The foundation of a successful safety training business is a clear understanding of the community you serve. Today, the demand for CPR and safety expertise is at an all-time high, as businesses and individuals alike recognize that being prepared is a vital life skill. By identifying your specific market early, you position yourself as a specialized authority rather than a generalist, allowing you to build a brand that resonates with impact and professionalism.

Identifying Your High-Value Audience

A thriving business is built on serving diverse groups with unique safety needs. You are providing the confidence to act, and your target audience includes anyone who values the protection of human life. Focus on these core segments to build a robust client base:

- **Healthcare & Professional Responders:** This includes nurses, dental hygienists, and therapists who require consistent certification to maintain their professional standing.

- **Corporate & Industrial Teams:** Modern workplaces prioritize safety compliance. From manufacturing plants to corporate offices, these clients look for streamlined training that meets regulatory standards.
- **Education & Childcare Providers:** Teachers, coaches, and daycare staff are the guardians of our communities and represent a consistent, recurring market for safety training.
- **Community & Civic Leaders:** Non-profits, faith-based organizations, and youth sports leagues often seek training to ensure the well-being of their members and volunteers.

Strategic Market Positioning

Effective market research allows you to tailor your programs to the specific preferences and "pain points" of your audience. By understanding the local landscape, you can identify which sectors are underserved and offer customized training solutions that meet them exactly where they are. This strategic approach ensures your marketing efforts are precise, efficient, and highly effective.

Action Steps:

- **Map Your Local Opportunities:** Identify the primary industries and large-scale employers in your area that require safety certifications.
- **Discover Emerging Needs:** Look for local safety trends or recent changes in community requirements that increase the demand for training.
- **Engage with Stakeholders:** Connect with local business owners or school administrators to learn about their specific safety goals for the coming year.
- **Leverage Insight Tools:** Utilize digital search data and local business directories to see where potential clients are searching for safety solutions in your region.

DAY 2: IDENTIFY APPROPRIATE LOCATIONS FOR CPR AND SAFETY TRAINING SESSIONS

A great location is the backbone of a professional training experience. In this industry, your space must be more than just convenient; it must be technically compliant and physically conducive to high-performance learning. Research from the American Heart Association indicates that high-quality chest compressions are the most significant factor in survival; therefore, your training environment must provide the space and comfort required to master this physical skill.

Step 1: Define Your Operational Model

Before securing a space, identify the "Format" of your business. This decision dictates your overhead and your daily schedule:

- **The 1-on-1 "Skills Check" Hub:** This model focuses on high-frequency, single-student sessions. Many healthcare professionals prefer "Blended Learning," where they complete the theory online and come to you for a

15-to-30-minute individual skills check. This requires minimal square footage (as little as **100–150 sq. ft.**) but high accessibility.

- **The Single-Classroom Boutique:** A dedicated home base (roughly **500 sq. ft.**) where you host groups of 6–12 students. This builds a consistent local "landmark" for your brand.
- **The Multi-Classroom Safety Center:** A larger facility with multiple rooms allowing for concurrent sessions (e.g., BLS in Room A, Heartsaver in Room B). This model is built for high-volume growth and hiring additional instructors.

Step 2: Strategic Location Options

Modern entrepreneurs have a variety of ways to establish a professional presence without the burden of a long-term, expensive lease. Consider these high-flexibility options:

- **Satellite Offices & Executive Suites:** Utilizing providers like **Regus, WeWork, or local professional centers** allows you to rent high-end meeting rooms by the hour or day. This gives you a prestigious "business district" address and professional lobby for your students at a fraction of the cost of a full lease.

- **The "Completely Mobile" Model:** This low-overhead approach focuses exclusively on **On-Site Corporate Training**. You bring the classroom to the client—boardrooms, warehouses, or staff breakrooms. This is highly attractive to B2B clients who want to train their entire staff at once without the logistical headache of employee travel.
- **Contractual Staffing:** In this model, you act as the safety partner for large organizations (like hospitals or school districts), providing the instructors to use *their* existing training rooms on a recurring basis.

The Science of the Professional Space

Regardless of the model you choose, ensure your space meets these professional metrics:

- **Spatial Optimization:** Aim for **35 to 45 square feet per student** to allow for dedicated mannequin stations and free movement.
- **Atmospheric Comfort:** High-quality compressions are physically demanding. A well-ventilated room set between **68°F and 72°F** ensures students can perform without exhaustion.

- **Illumination:** Ensure the space has clear, bright lighting (approx. **30 foot-candles**) so students can accurately see anatomical landmarks and AED prompts.

Action Steps:

- **Commit to a Model:** Decide if you will start as an Individual Hub, a Classroom Boutique, or a Mobile-First enterprise.
- **Audit Your Local "Flex Space":** Research local executive suites (like Regus) and compare their hourly rates to your projected class revenue.
- **Draft your "Mobile Kit" Inventory:** If you choose the mobile or staffing route, list the portable equipment (ultralite mannequins, wheeled cases) needed to transform any room into a classroom in under 15 minutes.
- **Calculate Your Capacity:** Determine your maximum class size based on the square footage of your chosen primary location or satellite options.

DAY 3: DECIDE ON CPR AND SAFETY TRAINING COURSE OFFERINGS

Strategic course selection is the engine that drives your revenue. In the safety industry, your offerings should align with the most rigorous standards—typically those set by the **American Heart Association (AHA)**, **Red Cross**, or **Health & Safety Institute (HSI)**. Statistics show that over **12 million people** are trained in CPR annually in the U.S. alone. By selecting the right mix of courses, you ensure your business captures its share of this essential market.

Mastering the Core Curriculum

A successful training business typically categorizes its offerings to meet specific legal and professional requirements. By diversifying your courses, you protect your business from market shifts:

- **Basic Life Support (BLS):** This is your "bread and butter" for the healthcare sector. Doctors, nurses, and dental professionals are required by law to maintain this certification, ensuring a consistent, recurring revenue stream every two years.

- **Heartsaver® / Community CPR & First Aid:** Designed for the general public and non-clinical workplaces (like OSHA-regulated construction sites or daycare centers). Statistics indicate that **70% of out-of-hospital cardiac arrests** happen at home; marketing this to families and local businesses taps into a massive emotional and practical need.
- **Bloodborne Pathogens (BBP):** Often an overlooked "add-on," this course is vital for the tattoo industry, custodial staff, and first responders. Offering BBP as a digital or add-on module can increase your per-student revenue by **15–20%** with almost zero additional overhead.
- **Pediatric Advanced Life Support (PALS) & ACLS:** If you have the clinical background, these advanced courses command the highest price points and attract specialized medical professionals.

The "Blended Learning" Advantage

Modern training is moving toward a **"Phygital" model**—a combination of online theory and in-person skills practice. Offering blended learning options can increase your profit margins significantly because:

- **Time Efficiency:** You can process a "Skills Session" in **20–30 minutes** compared to a 4-hour full classroom session.
- **Scalability:** You can serve more students per day without increasing your physical footprint.
- **Client Preference:** Busy professionals increasingly choose blended learning for its flexibility, with some providers reporting a **30% increase** in bookings when this option is available.

Action Steps:

- **Select Your Certifying Body:** Align with a nationally recognized organization (AHA, Red Cross, HSI) to ensure your certificates are accepted by all major employers.
- **Identify Your "Signature" Course:** Based on your Day 1 research, pick the one course that will be your primary focus (e.g., BLS for a town with many clinics).
- **Create Tiered Packages:** Develop "Safety Bundles" (e.g., CPR + First Aid + AED Training)

to provide comprehensive value and increase your average transaction size.

- **Research the "Skills-Only" Market:** Analyze local demand for blended learning skills checks to see if you can implement a "high-speed" session model.

Day 4: Decide on CPR And Safety Training Course Prices

A strategic pricing structure is the engine of a scalable seven-figure enterprise. Your pricing must reflect the high value of the life-saving skills you provide while remaining competitive in your local market. Research indicates that the average profit margin for a well-run CPR training business ranges from **50% to 70%**, depending on class size and overhead. By shifting from a "cost-covering" mindset to "value-based" pricing, you empower your business to grow with healthy, sustainable margins.

Benchmarking the Market Value

Industry data shows that professional certification costs vary based on the complexity of the course and the depth of the curriculum. Use these national averages as a foundation for your local strategy:

- **Community/Heartsaver® Courses:** Typically priced between **$60 and $100**. These are essential for the general public, teachers, and fitness professionals.

- **Basic Life Support (BLS):** Generally priced from **$80 to $125**. This is a mandatory requirement for healthcare providers, creating a "recession-proof" revenue stream.
- **Advanced Courses (ACLS/PALS):** High-level clinical certifications that command **$200 to $300+** per student.
- **Skills Sessions (Blended Learning):** Focused, 30-minute hands-on checks usually priced at **$50 to $75**. Because your time commitment is minimal, these often yield the highest hourly profit.

The Profitability Formula

To ensure your business thrives, your pricing must account for your **Cost of Goods Sold (COGS)**. A professional benchmark is to ensure your revenue per class is at least **2.5 to 3 times** your direct variable expenses.

Average Variable Costs per Student:

- **Certification Card Fee:** $5 – $25 (Varies by provider)
- **Student Materials/Manuals:** $5 – $15
- **Consumables (Wipes, Lung Bags):** $2 – $5

- **TOTAL VARIABLE COST:** Approximately **$12 – $45 per student**

High-Margin Corporate Strategies

For business-to-business (B2B) clients, shift from "per person" pricing to a **"Flat Rate"** model. This simplifies the sales process and guarantees your income regardless of student attendance.

- **The "Group 10" Rate:** Offer a flat fee for up to 10 students (e.g., $800–$1,000). This provides the client with a bulk discount while securing a high daily rate for your time.
- **Travel & Convenience Fees:** On-site training is a premium service. Adding a **$50–$150 mobile fee** for training at the client's location covers your logistics and positions your brand as a high-convenience partner.

Action Steps

- **Conduct a Competitive Audit:** Research 3–5 local competitors and list their prices for BLS and Heartsaver classes. Position your brand as the "Premium Value" choice.
- **Calculate Your Break-Even Point:** Determine exactly how many students you need per class

to cover your instructor pay, rent, and materials.

- **Develop a "Corporate Quote" Sheet:** Create a pricing menu for businesses that includes flat rates for groups of 10, 20, and 30+.
- **Review Pricing Semiannually:** Set a schedule to review your pricing every six months to stay aligned with increases in supply costs or regional demand.

DAY 5: DECIDE ON HOURS AND DAYS OF OPERATION

A strategic schedule is the foundation of a high-performance business. In the training industry, the most profitable hours are those that align with the "off-shift" needs of healthcare workers or the "production downtime" of corporate teams. Research into consumer booking habits shows that **over 40% of appointments are booked outside of standard business hours**, which means your hours of operation should be a strategic reflection of your community's needs.

Strategic Scheduling for Peak Profitability

To maximize your revenue, identify the specific "Buying Windows" of your target segments:

- **The Healthcare "Shift-Change" Window:** Medical professionals often seek certifications during their days off or between shift rotations. Offering early morning (7:00 AM) or mid-week sessions allows you to capture this dedicated market while competitors may be closed.

- **The Corporate "Down-Time" Block:**
  Business-to-business (B2B) clients typically prefer Tuesday, Wednesday, or Thursday between 9:00 AM and 2:00 PM. This avoids Monday morning planning and Friday afternoon departures, ensuring maximum employee attendance.
- **The Weekend "Community" Surge:** For the general public—including parents, students, and coaches—Saturday morning is the highest-demand period. Statistics show that weekend classes often see a **20% higher attendance rate** for non-professional certifications.
- **The "Gap-Fill" Skills Check:** By offering 30-minute "Skills Checks" during your office hours, you can fill the gaps between larger group classes, turning a slow Tuesday afternoon into a high-margin revenue block.

Leveraging Automation for 24/7 Bookings

In a professional safety business, your "Hours of Training" are different from your "Hours of Availability." By utilizing online booking platforms, your business is effectively "open" for sales 24/7. This self-service model is preferred by modern professionals and allows you to scale without needing a full-time receptionist.

Action Steps

- **Define Your Primary Training Blocks:** Based on your Day 1 research, set 3–4 consistent weekly time slots that align with your target audience's peak availability.
- **Identify Competitor "Gaps":** Research local training centers. If they are all closed on Sundays or evenings, consider offering a premium "After-Hours" session to capture that underserved market.
- **Establish a Registration Deadline:** To protect your profit margins, set a 24-to-48-hour registration cut-off. This ensures you only staff and prepare for classes that meet your minimum student count.
- **Implement Automated Reminders:** Use your scheduling system to send text and email reminders 24 hours before class. This simple step can reduce "no-shows" by up to **50%**, protecting your daily revenue.

DAY 6: CHOOSE A NAME

Choosing your business name is a pivotal step in establishing your identity as a market leader. Your name is the first touchpoint for your clients and a reflection of your brand's authority. A strong name does more than identify you; it communicates your mission and makes you easily discoverable in a digital-first marketplace. Research indicates that clear, descriptive names can lead to a **33% higher click-through rate** in local searches compared to abstract titles.

The Psychology of a Powerful Brand Name

In the safety and training industry, your name should inspire confidence and clarity. Aim for a name that meets these professional criteria:

- **Instant Clarity:** Within three seconds, a potential client should know exactly what you do. Including keywords like "CPR," "Safety," "Lifesaver," or "Training" ensures you are immediately categorized as an expert.
- **Memorability & Simplicity:** Brands with names that are easy to pronounce and spell are significantly more likely to be shared via

word-of-mouth. Avoid complex acronyms or creative spellings that might confuse a voice-activated search (like Siri or Alexa).

- **Local vs. Scalable:** Deciding whether to include your city name (e.g., "Atlanta CPR Pros") or a broader term (e.g., "Elite Safety Solutions") depends on your vision. Localized names often rank faster in search engines for their specific area, while broader names allow for easier expansion into multiple cities or states.
- **The Trust Factor:** Words that evoke reliability—such as "Certified," "Guardian," "Response," or "Vital"—help bridge the gap between a stranger and a loyal client.

SEO and Digital Ownership

Before finalizing your choice, it is vital to ensure you can own the digital space associated with that name. Studies show that **75% of users** never scroll past the first page of search results. A name that is unique enough to rank #1 for its own brand search is a massive asset.

Action Steps

- **Brainstorm with Strategy:** List 10 names that reflect your brand values. Use a mix of

"Descriptive" names (what you do) and "Evocative" names (how you make clients feel).

- **Conduct a Digital Availability Audit:** Check for available domain names (.com is the gold standard) and social media handles. Consistency across all platforms—from Instagram to LinkedIn—builds professional credibility.
- **Perform a Trademark & Secretary of State Search:** Verify that your chosen name is not already in use within your state or industry to avoid future legal hurdles.
- **Test for "Voice Search" Compatibility:** Say your business name out loud to a voice-assistant. If the technology struggles to understand or spell it, consider a simpler variation to ensure you remain discoverable in the modern era.

DAY 7: SET UP YOUR BUSINESS STRUCTURE & OPERATIONS

Establishing your business structure is a critical step in transitioning from an instructor to a CEO. Your legal entity is the framework that protects your personal assets, optimizes your tax strategy, and establishes professional credibility. According to the U.S. Small Business Administration, choosing the correct structure early can significantly reduce administrative friction as you scale.

Choosing Your Legal Foundation

The "right" structure depends on your vision for growth and your comfort with administrative requirements. Common paths for CPR and safety businesses include:

- **Limited Liability Company (LLC):** The most popular choice for training businesses. It provides personal asset protection—meaning your personal savings and home are shielded from business liabilities—while offering "pass-through" taxation that simplifies your filings.

- **S-Corporation:** As your business grows (typically once you exceed **$60,000–$75,000** in annual profit), an S-Corp election can offer significant savings on self-employment taxes by allowing you to pay yourself a "reasonable salary" and take remaining profits as distributions.
- **Professional Liability & Insurance:** In the safety industry, insurance is non-negotiable. General liability (covering accidents in class) typically costs around **$30/month**, while Professional Liability (Errors & Omissions) protects you if a student claims they were taught incorrectly.

Streamlining Daily Operations

A successful business is a "system of systems." To ensure you can scale without burning out, you must define how your business breathes every day.

- **Registration Flow:** Use automated platforms to handle the journey from "interested lead" to "paid student."
- **Certification Fulfillment:** Set a goal to issue digital eCards within **24 hours** of class completion.

- **Manikin Maintenance:** Establish a standard cycle for decontaminating **manikins** and checking AED trainer batteries to ensure equipment is always "audit-ready."

Action Steps

- **Select Your Legal Entity:** Consult with a professional to determine if a single-member LLC or an S-Corp election fits your 12-month revenue goals.
- **Obtain Your EIN:** Register for a Federal Employer Identification Number (EIN) with the IRS. This is required to open a business bank account and hire future instructors.
- **File Your Articles of Organization:** Complete your registration with your Secretary of State to officially recognize your business as a legal entity.
- **Secure Professional Insurance:** Obtain quotes for General and Professional Liability insurance to ensure you are covered before your first student walks through the door.

Day 8: Develop a Business Plan & Secure Funding

Developing a comprehensive business plan is the process of mapping your vision into a measurable reality. A well-structured plan acts as a living roadmap for your growth and is a prerequisite for securing capital from lenders or investors. Research indicates that entrepreneurs who craft a formal business plan are **16% more likely** to achieve long-term viability. This document proves that you aren't just an instructor; you are a high-level strategist building a sustainable enterprise.

The Anatomy of a Profitable Plan

To attract funding or partnerships, your business plan should highlight the "Success Drivers" of the safety industry:

- **Executive Summary:** A high-impact overview of your mission to increase community survival rates and build a profitable training hub.

- **Market Analysis:** Data-driven evidence of the high demand for certifications among local healthcare and corporate sectors.
- **Operational Strategy:** Detailing your "system of systems," including your use of automated scheduling and high-quality **manikins** for superior student outcomes.
- **Financial Projections:** A clear 3-to-5-year forecast showing how diverse revenue streams—like course fees, AED sales, and corporate contracts—will drive your growth.

Calculating Your Launch Capital

Starting a CPR business is uniquely cost-effective, but "Smart Capital" can accelerate your launch. On average, a professional solo-instructor startup requires an initial investment of **$2,500 to $5,000**.

Estimated Core Startup Costs:

- **Instructor Certification & Fees:** $500 – $1,000
- **Initial Training Kit:** $1,500 – $3,500 (Includes a 4-pack of adult **manikins**, 2 infant **manikins**, and 2 AED trainers)
- **Legal & Insurance:** $500 – $1,500 (LLC formation and initial liability premiums)
- **Marketing & Website:** $500 – $1,000

Securing Funding for Growth

- **SBA Microloans:** The Small Business Administration offers specialized loans for small-scale startups, often providing better rates than traditional banks for equipment like feedback-enabled **manikins**.
- **Equipment Financing:** Many safety supply vendors offer "Buy Now, Pay Later" programs, allowing you to pay for your gear using the revenue generated from your first few classes.
- **Corporate Sponsorships:** Local insurance companies or hospitals may provide "safety grants" to help you launch programs that lower community risk.
- **Federal Training Grants:** Programs like the **Susan Harwood Training Grant** (OSHA) provide funding for organizations specifically delivering workplace safety and health training.

Action Steps

- **Draft Your "Pitch Deck":** Create a 10-slide visual summary of your business plan that highlights your unique value proposition and projected profit margins.

- **Itemize Your Asset List:** List every piece of equipment needed—from **manikins** to AED trainers—to determine your exact "Break-Even" point.
- **Research Local SBDC Resources:** Connect with your local Small Business Development Center for free mentoring on refining your financial projections.
- **Apply for a Business Credit Card:** Start building a separate credit profile for your business to simplify expense tracking and secure future lines of credit.

DAY 9: OBTAIN NECESSARY LICENSES & CERTIFICATIONS

Securing the proper credentials is the moment your business gains its legal and professional "teeth." In the safety industry, licenses and certifications are your "Seal of Excellence," providing the peace of mind clients need to trust your brand. By diversifying your certifications beyond CPR, you tap into a broader market: research shows that the **global safety training market** is expanding as regulatory requirements for driver, food, and workplace safety become more stringent worldwide.

Building a Multi-Vertical Certification Strategy

To become a "One-Stop Safety Shop," you must align with the specific regulatory bodies governing each field:

- **CPR & Medical Training:** Align with the **American Heart Association (AHA)** or **Red Cross**. These are the "gold standard" for healthcare and childcare providers.

- **Food Safety & Sanitation:** Obtain instructor status through **ServSafe** or similar ANSI-accredited programs. These certifications are mandatory for restaurant managers and food handlers in nearly every state, providing a high-volume, recurring revenue stream.
- **Driver & Fleet Safety:** Partner with the **National Safety Council (NSC)** or specialized driver safety organizations. Companies with vehicle fleets often require annual defensive driving certifications to lower their insurance premiums.
- **Workplace & OSHA Compliance:** Consider becoming an **OSHA Outreach Trainer**. This allows you to issue 10-hour and 30-hour cards for construction and general industry, which are highly lucrative corporate contracts.

The Trust Factor: Licensing and Credentialing

When a client sees that you are "Licensed, Insured, and Multi-Certified," you move from being a "tutor" to a "compliance partner."

- **State & Local Business Licenses:** Most municipalities require a general business license. If you are operating a fixed facility, you may also need a **Certificate of Occupancy** that permits "educational services."

- **Instructor Portals:** Once certified, you gain access to secure portals (like the AHA Instructor Network or the ServSafe portal) to order student materials and issue digital, verifiable certificates instantly.

Action Steps

- **Map Out Your "Certification Roadmap":** Prioritize certifications based on local demand—start with CPR/BLS, then layer in Food Safety or Driver Safety based on your Day 1 market research.
- **Complete Professional Onboarding:** Enroll in the "Instructor Essentials" or "Train-the-Trainer" modules for your chosen disciplines.
- **Verify Eligibility and Prerequisites:** Many advanced safety certifications require a baseline of experience (e.g., a background in food service for ServSafe or a clean driving record for Driver Safety).
- **Confirm Alignment with a Training Center:** For CPR, ensure you are formally "aligned" with a Training Center that can process your rosters and issue student eCards efficiently.

Day 10: Choose the Right Equipment & Supplies

Selecting your equipment is one of the most significant investments you will make in your business. High-quality **manikins** and training tools act as silent co-instructors, providing real-time data that helps students correct their form instantly. Statistics show that feedback-driven training increases the retention of life-saving skills by over **25%** compared to traditional methods. By investing in modern, 2026-compliant equipment, you position your brand as a high-tech, premium provider.

The Essential "Safety Solution" Kit

To serve your diverse client base—from healthcare workers to restaurant managers—you need a versatile inventory:

- **High-Tech CPR Manikins:** Ensure your adult and infant manikins feature **integrated feedback monitors**. These provide visual (lights) and audio (clicks) cues to confirm students are hitting the 100–120 compressions-per-minute target.

- **AED Trainers:** Unlike live AEDs, these trainers simulate various cardiac arrest scenarios without delivering a shock. Aim for at least **one trainer for every two students** to maximize hands-on time.
- **Specialized Training Tools:**
  - **Food Safety:** Digital thermometers, ATP swabs (for surface testing), and glow-germ kits for handwashing demonstrations.
  - **Driver Safety:** Vision impairment goggles ("drunk goggles") and digital reaction-time simulators to provide a vivid, impactful learning experience.
  - **First Aid & Bleeding Control:** Tourniquet trainers and wound-packing simulators are high-demand items for modern corporate "Stop the Bleed" sessions.

Sourcing for Profitability

Smart purchasing reduces your overhead and increases your long-term margins. Use these industry benchmarks to guide your budget:

- **The "Starter Set" Benchmark:** A professional 4-pack of feedback-enabled adult manikins and AED trainers typically costs between **$1,200 and $1,500.**

- **Consumables Management:** Budget for high-volume items like manikin lung bags (**$1–$2 each**) and face shields. Buying these in bulk can reduce your per-student cost by up to **30%.**
- **Vendor Loyalty:** Establish a relationship with a primary supplier like **Prestan, Laerdal, or specialized safety distributors**. Many offer "Instructor Discounts" or tiered pricing as your order volume increases.

Action Steps:

- **Audit for 2026 Compliance:** Ensure all manikins meet the latest **instrumented directive feedback** requirements (rate, depth, and chest recoil).
- **Inventory Your "Mobile Kit":** If you are offering on-site training, invest in wheeled, padded carrying cases to protect your manikins and technology during transport.
- **Create a Maintenance Log:** Establish a routine to decontaminate manikins after every class and replace AED trainer batteries quarterly to avoid equipment failure during a session.

- **Shop "Bundled" Packages:** Look for "Instructor Starter Kits" that bundle manikins, trainers, and consumables together; these typically offer a **10–15% savings** over individual item purchases.

DAY 11: DESIGN YOUR LOGO AND CHOOSE A TAGLINE

Your brand identity is the visual promise you make to your customers. In an industry centered on emergency response and compliance, your logo and tagline must radiate authority, reliability, and calm. Consistent branding doesn't just look professional; it can increase your revenue by **up to 20%** by building the recognition required to secure large-scale corporate contracts in driver, food, and medical safety.

The Psychology of Safety Branding

To create a logo that resonates with both healthcare professionals and business owners, utilize the proven emotional triggers of color and shape:

- **The Power of Blue:** Used by **33% of the world's top brands**, blue is the universal color of trust, stability, and professionalism. It is the gold standard for medical and safety training businesses.
- **The "Vitality" of Green:** Green represents health, growth, and safety (think of a green

traffic light). It is an excellent choice for a business that offers **food safety** and wellness-focused courses.

- **The Urgency of Red:** While red can signal "danger," when used as an accent (like in a heart or a cross), it creates a sense of vital importance and immediate action—perfect for **CPR and first aid**.
- **Clean Typography:** Use bold, sans-serif fonts (like Helvetica or Montserrat). These are perceived as modern, clean, and "no-nonsense," which is exactly the vibe you want for a compliance-based business.

Crafting a High-Impact Tagline

A tagline for a safety business should be more than a "catchy phrase." It should be a **Safety Slogan** that reinforces your mission. Effective safety taglines typically fall into three categories:

1. **Results-Oriented:** "Training for Life," "Because Seconds Count," or "Certifying Tomorrow's Heroes."
2. **Compliance-Focused:** "Your Partner in Workplace Safety," "Compliance Made Simple," or "Expert Training, Guaranteed Results."

3. **Broad Safety Coverage:** "Safety Solutions for Home, Road, and Kitchen" (perfect if you offer **driver** and **food safety**).

Action Steps

- **Brainstorm with Keywords:** List 10 words that describe your business (e.g., *Shield, Heart, Expert, Swift, Secure*). Use these to guide your visual icons.
- **Create a "Trust" Mood Board:** Gather images of the colors and fonts used by the "Big Three" (AHA, Red Cross, NSC) to ensure your brand feels like it belongs in the same elite category.
- **Test for Scalability:** Ensure your logo looks just as good on a small business card as it does on a large manikin carrying case or a highway billboard for your **driver safety** program.
- **Finalize Your "Elevator Pitch" Tagline:** Say your tagline out loud. If it takes more than 3 seconds to say or is hard to understand over the phone, simplify it. Aim for a "short, punchy, and protective" feel.

Day 12: Design Your CPR And Safety Training Website

Your website is the digital storefront of your safety enterprise. In an industry driven by urgent certification needs, a high-performing site must do three things: provide instant credibility, rank high in local searches, and convert visitors into paid students in under 60 seconds. Research indicates that **75% of users** judge a company's credibility based on its website design. For a business that teaches life-saving skills, a clean, modern, and mobile-responsive site is non-negotiable.

Navigating Trademark & Logo Permissions

To build trust, you will want to showcase the organizations you are certified to teach (like the AHA, Red Cross, or ServSafe). However, **you must have explicit permission to use their logos.** Each organization has strict "Brand Identity Guidelines" that dictate how their logo can appear.

- **Check Your Instructor Agreement:** Most certifying bodies provide a specific

"Authorized Provider" or "Instructor" logo that is different from their main corporate logo.

- **Avoid "Logo Soup":** Never download a logo from a Google image search. Instead, log in to your Instructor Portal (e.g., the AHA Instructor Network or the Red Cross Learning Center) to download the approved "Instructor" or "Training Site" digital assets.
- **Mandatory Disclaimers:** Many organizations require a specific text disclaimer on your website (e.g., *"The American Heart Association strongly promotes knowledge and proficiency in all AHA courses and has developed instructional materials for this purpose..."*). Including this protects you from trademark infringement.

The "High-Conversion" Website Architecture

To serve a diverse client base—from a nurse needing BLS to a fleet manager needing **driver safety**—your site should be organized into clear "Conversion Paths":

- **The Instant Booking Engine:** Use a 24/7 self-service scheduling tool. Statistics show that **82% of customers** prefer booking online rather than calling.

- **Segmented Service Pages:** Create dedicated landing pages for each vertical to boost your SEO:
  - **Medical & Community:** CPR, AED, and First Aid.
  - **Industrial & Fleet: Driver Safety** and OSHA compliance.
  - **Hospitality: Food Safety** (ServSafe) and Alcohol Awareness.
- **The "Social Proof" Section:** Feature testimonials from local businesses you have trained. This reduces "buyer friction" and establishes you as the local safety authority.

Action Steps

- **Download Official Brand Assets:** Log in to your various instructor portals to secure the approved logos for your website. Do not use the "main" corporate logo unless you have a specific partnership agreement.
- **Insert Required Disclaimers:** Place the mandatory certifying body disclaimers in your website footer or on your "About" page to remain in full compliance.
- **Optimize for Local SEO:** Use keywords like "CPR Certification [Your City]" and "Food

Safety Class [Your City]" to ensure you rank #1 when local clients are searching for training.

- **Test the Mobile Experience:** Ensure your "Book Now" buttons are easy to click on a smartphone. Over **60% of web traffic** in 2026 is mobile, and a clumsy mobile site will cost you registrations.

Day 13: Open Business Bank Account And Accept Online Payments

Establishing a dedicated business bank account is the "Great Wall" that protects your personal assets from your business liabilities. In the safety industry—where you manage high-volume certifications and equipment—financial clarity is your best tool for scaling. By 2026, automated payment systems have become the standard; businesses that offer frictionless, one-click payment options are perceived as more professional and trustworthy by both individual students and corporate clients.

The Power of Financial Separation

Separating your accounts isn't just about organization; it's about **legal protection and tax efficiency**:

- **Asset Protection:** Keeping your personal and business funds in separate "buckets" reinforces your LLC or Corporate structure, ensuring your personal home and savings aren't at risk during a business dispute.

- **Audit-Proof Bookkeeping:** During tax season, having a clean, business-only statement allows you to identify every deduction—from manikin lung bags to driver safety software—without sifting through personal grocery receipts.
- **Building Business Credit:** A dedicated account with a healthy transaction history is the primary document lenders look for when you're ready to secure a line of credit for expansion or a new training vehicle.

Modern Payment Solutions for 2026

Your customers expect a checkout experience that is as fast as the life-saving skills you teach.

- **The "One-Click" Standard:** Integrate processors like **Stripe** or **Square** with your booking site to accept **Apple Pay, Google Pay, and digital wallets**. These methods can reduce checkout friction by up to **40%**.
- **ACH & "Pay by Bank":** For large corporate contracts (like training a fleet of drivers or an entire restaurant staff), offering ACH bank transfers can save you thousands in credit card fees. Processing a $2,000 corporate

invoice via ACH typically costs pennies compared to a $60 credit card fee.

- **Buy Now, Pay Later (BNPL):** For higher-ticket certifications like ACLS or multi-day safety seminars, offering BNPL options (like Affirm or Klarna) allows students to pay in installments while you receive the full payment upfront.

Action Steps

- **Choose a High-Yield Business Account:** Look for banks like **Bluevine or American Express Business Checking**, which in 2026 offer up to **2.0% APY** on your operating balance, letting your cash work for you.
- **Gather Your Legal "ID" Bundle:** To open your account, you will need your **Employer Identification Number (EIN)**, your **Articles of Organization**, and your **Operating Agreement**.
- **Automate Your Invoicing:** Set up a system (like QuickBooks or FreshBooks) that automatically sends receipts and "Refresher Course" reminders. This turns a one-time student into a recurring revenue source every two years.
- **Enable "Invisible" Payments:** Ensure your website's registration flow is "invisible"—meaning the student pays as part

of the sign-up process so you never have to "chase" a payment on the day of class.

Day 14: Prepare A Budget And Open A Set Of Books

A well-structured budget is your business's financial GPS. In the safety training industry, successful businesses typically aim for a **50% to 70% profit margin**, but reaching these numbers requires a focus on tracking your **Cost of Goods Sold (COGS)**. By setting up your "books" correctly, you ensure you can track the ROI of every manikin and every marketing dollar spent.

Building Your "Safety First" Budget

To ensure profitability across all your verticals—including CPR, **driver safety**, and **food safety**—your budget should reflect these established startup figures:

Initial Startup Capital ($2,500 – $5,000)

- **Instructor Certification & Fees:** $500 – $1,000
- **Initial Training Kit:** $1,500 – $3,500 (4-pack adult **manikins**, 2 infant **manikins**, 2 AED trainers)
- **Legal & Insurance:** $500 – $1,500 (LLC formation and initial premiums)

- **Marketing & Website:** $500 – $1,000

Variable Costs (Per–Student)

- **Certification Fees:** $5 – $25 (eCards)
- **Supplies:** Student manuals, lung bags, and sanitizing wipes.

Fixed Monthly Operations

- **Software:** Website hosting and scheduling tools.
- **Insurance:** Professional liability premiums.

Choosing Your Accounting Method

Most new safety businesses use the **Cash Basis** method because it is simple: you record income when you receive it and expenses when you pay them.

- **QuickBooks Online:** Best for overall growth and hiring instructors.
- **FreshBooks:** Best for invoicing corporate clients for **food or driver safety** sessions.
- **Wave:** A powerful, budget-friendly option for solo entrepreneurs.

Action Steps

- **Establish Your "Burn Rate":** Calculate the exact monthly cost to keep your business running. This tells you the minimum number of students needed to break even.
- **Open Cloud-Based Accounting:** Connect your business bank account to your software so transactions are automatically categorized. This reduces tax-season stress.
- **Create a "Manikin Depreciation" Fund:** Set aside a small percentage of every class fee. This ensures you have cash ready to upgrade your equipment without needing a loan.
- **Monitor Your Cash Runway:** Aim to keep **3 to 6 months** of operating expenses in reserve to weather slow months or invest in new training verticals.

Day 15: Set Up And Optimize Social Media

Social media is more than a place to post photos; it is a high-speed referral engine. For a business offering diverse services like CPR, **driver safety**, and **food safety**, different platforms allow you to target specific audiences: Facebook for local families, LinkedIn for corporate safety officers, and Instagram for behind-the-scenes authority.

Platform Strategy: Target Your Audience

Don't try to be everywhere at once. Focus on where your specific high-value clients spend their time:

- **Facebook (Local & Community):** The best tool for filling community CPR classes. Join local community groups and share safety tips. Use Facebook's "Events" feature to list your upcoming classes so neighbors can find them easily.
- **LinkedIn (Corporate & B2B):** This is where you win contracts for **driver safety** and **food safety**. Connect with HR managers, operations directors, and fleet supervisors. Share articles

on "Reducing Workplace Liability" or "The Cost of Non-Compliance" to position yourself as a consultant, not just an instructor.

- **Instagram & TikTok (Visual Authority):** Perfect for short, 30-second "Safety Hacks." Show a quick demo of how to use a feedback-enabled manikin or a "pro-tip" for checking food temperatures. This "humanizes" your brand and builds instant trust.

Content That Converts

In the safety industry, "educational content" is your strongest marketing tool. Follow the **80/20 Rule**: 80% of your posts should be helpful/educational, and only 20% should be direct "sales" posts.

- **The "Save Story":** Share (with permission) stories of students who used their training in real life. Nothing sells a safety course better than proof that it works.
- **Safety "Myth-Busters":** Address common misconceptions, like "Should you put butter on a burn?" (No!) or "Is it okay to drive while tired if the windows are down?" (No!).
- **Equipment Spotlights:** Show off your high-tech **manikins** and AED trainers. Explain

why you use the best gear to provide the best
training.

Action Steps

- **Claim Your Handles:** Secure your business
  name across Facebook, Instagram, and
  LinkedIn to ensure brand consistency.
- **Optimize Your Bio:** Your bio should be a
  "mini-pitch." Example: *"Helping [City Name]
  stay safe. Certified CPR, Driver Safety, and
  Food Safety training for individuals & teams.
  Book below!* 👇 *"*
- **Set a Posting Schedule:** Aim for **3 posts per
  week.** Use a free tool like Buffer or the Meta
  Business Suite to schedule your posts in
  advance so you can stay focused on teaching.
- **Engage Locally:** Spend 10 minutes a day
  commenting on posts from local businesses,
  hospitals, and restaurants. This "digital
  networking" makes your brand a familiar face
  in the community.

Day 16: Use Pictures To Boost Your Business

In the safety industry, a picture isn't just worth a thousand words—it's worth a thousand "trust points." High-quality visuals bridge the gap between a student's fear of the unknown and their confidence to book a class. Whether you are showcasing your high-tech **manikins**, a clean training environment, or a professional **driver safety** simulation, your imagery tells the story of your expertise before you ever speak a word.

Visual Cues for Credibility

To appeal to healthcare professionals and corporate decision-makers, your photos must radiate professionalism and clinical accuracy:

- **Equipment in Action:** Take clear, well-lit photos of your feedback-enabled **manikins**. Highlight the visual monitors or lights that show students are performing correct compressions. This proves you use modern, compliant technology.

- **The "Environment" Shot:** Show your training space. Whether it's a fixed classroom or a mobile setup at a corporate office, a tidy, organized space signals that you are a serious professional.
- **Vertical-Specific Imagery:**
  - **Driver Safety:** Use photos of your reaction-time simulators or vision-impairment goggles.
  - **Food Safety:** Capture high-resolution shots of professional-grade thermometers and sanitation tools.
- **The Human Connection:** Photos of students (with permission) engaged and smiling while practicing on **manikins** remove the "intimidation factor" of safety training.

Photography Compliance & Best Practices

In a medical-adjacent field, how you take and share photos matters for both your brand and your legal protection:

- **HIPAA & Privacy Awareness:** When taking photos of "simulated" medical scenes, ensure no real personal information or sensitive data is visible in the background.

- **Model Releases:** Always get a signed simple photo release form if you feature students or staff in your marketing.
- **Authenticity Over Stock:** While stock photos are okay for blog posts, use **real photos** of your gear and your team on your homepage. Authenticity increases conversion rates by **up to 35%**.
- **Lighting is Everything:** Use soft, natural light or simple ring lights to avoid harsh shadows on your equipment. A clear, bright photo of a **manikin** looks professional; a dark, blurry one looks like a hobby.

Action Steps

- **Conduct a "Brand Shoot":** Spend two hours setting up your best **manikins**, AED trainers, and safety manuals. Take 20 high-quality photos from various angles.
- **Capture "The Details":** Take close-up shots of the feedback monitors on your **manikins**. These small details reinforce your commitment to 2026 compliance standards.
- **Update Your Google Business Profile:** Upload at least 5 of your new photos to your Google Profile. Profiles with photos receive **94% more views** than those without.

- **Create a "Photo Consent" Checkbox:** Add a small line to your digital registration form asking students if they consent to being photographed for social media. This automates your legal "paperwork."

Day 17: Create A Content Calendar

A content calendar is the "Syllabus" for your brand's online education. Instead of waking up and wondering what to post, a calendar allows you to align your marketing with seasonal safety trends and compliance cycles. By planning ahead, you ensure that you are consistently visible to families looking for CPR, restaurants needing **food safety**, and businesses requiring **driver safety** training.

Seasonal Safety Themes

To keep your content fresh and relevant, align your posts with national safety observances throughout the year. This makes your business part of a larger conversation:

- **January:** New Year, New Skills (Focus on resolution-based training)
- **February:** American Heart Month (The "Super Bowl" for CPR instructors)
- **April:** Distracted Driving Awareness Month (Perfect for promoting **driver safety**)
- **May:** National Nurses & Teachers Month (Targeted certification refreshers)

- **June:** National Safety Month (A great time for general workplace safety audits)
- **July:** UV & Heat Safety (Focus on hydration and outdoor heatstroke prevention)
- **September:** National Preparedness Month (Focus on disaster kits and emergency planning)
- **October:** Fire Safety Month & Global Handwashing Day (A natural fit for **food safety**)
- **December:** National Handwashing Awareness Week & Winter Driving Safety

The "Diversified" Content Mix

To engage your different customer bases, vary your posts using this simple "Weekly Rhythm":

1. **Monday: The Pro-Tip.** A 30-second video demo (e.g., "The correct depth for infant chest compressions" or "How to check a food thermometer's accuracy").
2. **Wednesday: The Compliance Check.** A post for business owners (e.g., "Is your fleet compliant with local driver safety standards?" or "Does your kitchen have a certified food manager on every shift?").

3. **Friday: The Student Spotlight.** A photo of your latest class with their certificates or a testimonial from a satisfied corporate client.
4. **Sunday: The Schedule Drop.** A quick list of your upcoming open-enrollment classes for the next two weeks.

Action Steps

- **Pick Your Tool:** Use a simple digital calendar (Google Calendar) or a dedicated scheduling tool like **Buffer, Hootsuite, or Meta Business Suite**.
- **Plot the "Big Three":** Mark Heart Month (February), Distracted Driving Month (April), and Food Safety Month (September) as your "High-Promotion" periods.
- **Batch Your Content:** Spend 2 hours once a month filming all your short video tips and writing your captions. This prevents marketing from getting in the way of your actual training.
- **Monitor and Adjust:** Check your "Insights" once a month. If your **driver safety** tips are getting more "Shares" than your CPR posts, consider increasing the frequency of your driving content to match what your audience wants.

Day 18: Search Engine Optimization

SEO is your "digital megaphone." For a local safety business, it ensures that when a nurse searches for "CPR near me" or a restaurant owner looks for "food safety certification," **your** business is the first one they see. In the safety industry, ranking at the top isn't just about traffic—it's about establishing **E-E-A-T** (Experience, Expertise, Authoritativeness, and Trustworthiness).

The "Local Pack" Strategy

Since your business serves a specific geographic area, your most valuable real estate is the **Google Local Map Pack** (the top 3 business listings shown on a map). To dominate this space:

- **Google Business Profile (GBP):** This is your most important SEO tool. Ensure your name, address, and phone number (NAP) are 100% identical on your website and your GBP.
- **The Power of Reviews:** Aim for a steady stream of fresh, 5-star reviews. Google rewards businesses that interact with their customers, so make sure you respond to every review—positive or negative—within 48 hours.

- **Local Photos:** Regularly upload high-quality photos of your training kit, your classroom, and your team. Photos with local landmarks or "behind-the-scenes" action on **manikins** tell Google you are active in the community.

Keyword Targeting for Multiple Verticals

Don't just target "CPR." Use "long-tail keywords" that describe exactly what people are searching for. These often have less competition and higher conversion rates:

- **Medical/Community:** "BLS for Healthcare Providers [City Name]," "Infant CPR classes for parents [City Name]," "AHA vs Red Cross CPR [City Name]."
- **Driver Safety:** "Defensive driving course for fleet drivers," "Insurance reduction driving class [City Name]," "Teen driver safety training."
- **Food Safety:** "ServSafe Manager certification [City Name]," "Food handler card online vs in-person," "Restaurant health compliance training."

Technical & On-Page Essentials

- **Mobile-First Design:** Most local searches happen on smartphones. If your site doesn't load in under 3 seconds or is hard to navigate on a phone, Google will penalize your ranking.
- **Header Tags (H1, H2, H3):** Use your keywords in your headers. Your main title (H1) should clearly state what you do: *"Expert CPR and Safety Training in [Your City]."*
- **Meta Descriptions:** Write a 155-character "ad" for each page. Example: *"Get your AHA CPR certification in [City]! Small classes, feedback-enabled manikins, and same-day eCards. Book your seat today!"*

Action Steps

- **Claim & Verify Your Google Business Profile:** If you haven't yet, go to `business.google.com` and follow the verification steps immediately.
- **Run a Local Keyword Audit:** Use a free tool like **Google Keyword Planner** to see what people in your specific zip codes are typing into search bars.
- **Embed a Google Map:** Place a live Google Map on your "Contact" or "Locations" page. This helps Google connect your website to your physical service area.

- **Create "Location Pages":** If you serve multiple suburbs or cities, create a dedicated page for each (e.g., "Safety Training in [City A]" and "Safety Training in [City B]").

Day 19: Obtain Business Insurance

In the safety industry, your expertise is your product, but it is also your greatest liability. Whether you are teaching a student how to perform chest compressions on a **manikin**, instructing a fleet on **driver safety**, or certifying a kitchen manager in **food safety**, insurance is what prevents a single mistake or misunderstanding from becoming a financial disaster.

Why Instructors Need Specific Coverage

Even with perfect instruction, accidents happen. A student might injure themselves during a hands-on exercise, or a client might claim that your "bad advice" led to a workplace accident. Standard business insurance often isn't enough; you need policies tailored to the risks of an educator.

The "Big Three" Policies for Safety Training

- **Professional Liability (Errors & Omissions):** This is your "Malpractice" insurance. It protects you if a student claims you taught a technique incorrectly or failed to cover a critical safety protocol.

- ○ *Average Cost:* ~$30 to $65 per month.
- **General Liability:** This covers "slip and fall" accidents or property damage. If a student trips over a **manikin** case in your classroom or you accidentally damage a client's floor during on-site training, this policy steps in.
  - ○ *Average Cost:* ~$30 to $45 per month.
- **Commercial Auto Insurance:** If you are a mobile instructor traveling to corporate offices to teach **driver safety** or CPR, your personal auto insurance likely will not cover accidents that occur while you are "on the clock" with a car full of equipment.

The "BOP" Benefit

Many insurers offer a **Business Owner's Policy (BOP)**, which bundles General Liability and Property insurance into one discounted package. This is often the most cost-effective way to protect your business assets, like your high-tech **manikins** and AED trainers, from theft or fire.

Action Steps

- **Gather Your Details:** Have your projected annual revenue, number of students, and a list of your training equipment (including the value of your **manikins**) ready for the application.

- **Check Certifying Body Requirements:** Organizations like the American Heart Association (AHA) often require you to carry at least **$1 million per occurrence** in professional liability and may ask to be named as an "Additional Insured."
- **Get At Least Three Quotes:** Use specialized providers like **Insureon, Hiscox, or CM&F Group**, which have specific departments for CPR and safety instructors.
- **Secure Your "COI":** Once you pay your premium, download your **Certificate of Insurance (COI)** immediately. You will need to show this to corporate clients and landlords before you can begin training.

Day 20: Prepare Employee Handbook And Contracts For Contractors

As your safety business grows, you will eventually move from being a solo instructor to managing a team. In the safety industry, your staff—whether they are W-2 employees or 1099 independent contractors—are the face of your brand. Clear documentation ensures that every student, whether in a CPR, **driver safety**, or **food safety** class, receives the same high-quality, compliant experience.

Employee vs. Contractor: The Legal Distinction

Misclassifying workers is a common and costly mistake. It is vital to understand the difference to ensure you are meeting tax and labor law requirements:

- **W-2 Employees:** You control when, where, and how they work. You provide the equipment (manikins, AED trainers) and withhold taxes. They are ideal for consistent, long-term growth.

- **1099 Independent Contractors:** They often own their own equipment and choose which jobs to accept. You pay them a flat fee for a specific class. They are perfect for handling "overflow" classes or specialized training like **driver safety**.

The Essential "Safety Instructor" Contract

Every contractor or employee should sign a formal agreement that protects your business. Key clauses should include:

- **Standard of Care:** A requirement to teach strictly according to the latest guidelines (e.g., AHA, Red Cross, or NSC standards).
- **Professional Appearance:** Standards for dress (e.g., branded polos, no open-toed shoes) to maintain a clinical, professional image.
- **Non-Solicitation:** Prevents instructors from "taking" your corporate clients (like restaurants or trucking fleets) to start their own training service.
- **Insurance Requirements:** For 1099 contractors, require proof of their own Professional Liability insurance, often naming your company as an "Additional Insured."

The Employee Handbook: Your Quality Manual

A handbook isn't just about "rules"—it's a roadmap for success. For a safety training business, your handbook should detail:

- **Equipment Care:** Strict protocols for decontaminating **manikins** and checking AED trainer batteries after every session.
- **Incident Reporting:** What to do if a student is injured during a physical skills test or if a piece of equipment fails.
- **Certification Processing:** Clear deadlines for submitting rosters so students receive their eCards within 24–48 hours.
- **Brand Voice:** How to interact with students to make training engaging and stress-free rather than intimidating.

Action Steps

- **Define Your Hiring Strategy:** Determine if your first hire will be a 1099 contractor for flexibility or a W-2 employee for more control.
- **Draft a "Master" Instructor Agreement:** Include specific compliance clauses regarding the

certifying bodies (AHA, Red Cross, etc.) you represent.

- **Create an Equipment Checklist:** Add this to your handbook to ensure every instructor leaves the training site with the same number of **manikins** and supplies they brought.
- **Consult a Legal Professional:** Have a local employment attorney review your handbook and contracts to ensure they meet your specific state's labor laws.

Day 21: Build Your Team of Trainers & Instructors

As your business expands from community classes to large corporate contracts, your instructors become your most valuable assets. In the safety industry, the "gold standard" for hiring involves recruiting active or retired first responders—paramedics, firefighters, and nurses. Their real-world experience provides the clinical authority that keeps students engaged and confident.

Strategic Sourcing: Finding the Right Talent

Don't limit your search to standard job boards. In the safety training community, collaboration is often better than competition:

- **Network with Other Training Companies:** Reach out to local CPR and safety training centers. Many have high-quality instructors looking for extra contract hours to fill their schedules. Building a "mutual referral" relationship can help both businesses handle overflow during busy certification cycles.

- **Direct Web Presence:** Create a dedicated "Join Our Team" or "Careers" page on your website. Even when you aren't actively hiring, having an evergreen application form allows you to build a database of certified trainers for future needs.
- **Target First Responders:** Post on local EMS/Fire Department bulletin boards or nursing forums. These professionals already have the credentials and the "street cred" that students trust.

Tech-Savvy Instruction

Your team must be comfortable using modern tools to maintain your professional image:

- **Feedback Technology:** Instructors should be experts at explaining data from feedback-enabled **manikins** to help students achieve mastery.
- **Digital Check-In:** Use your mobile booking app to have instructors check in students on-site. This ensures your rosters are accurate and digital eCards can be issued immediately after class.

Onboarding for Brand Consistency

Your team represents your brand's "Safety Standard." Every instructor should go through a structured onboarding process:

- **The "Shadow" Phase:** New hires should observe at least two of your classes to learn your "Brand Voice" and how you handle specific student questions.
- **The "Monitored" Session:** Before they lead a class solo, you should monitor them teaching a full course to ensure they follow the latest AHA, NSC, or ANSI guidelines.
- **Contractor (1099) vs. Employee (W-2):** Many trainers prefer the flexibility of 1099 status, especially if they own their own gear. If you hire contractors, ensure your **Contractor Agreement** (from Day 20) is signed and their insurance certificates are on file.

Action Steps

- **Launch Your "Careers" Page:** Add a simple form to your website where instructors can upload their certifications and resumes.
- **Call Three Local Competitors:** Introduce yourself and ask if they have any instructors interested in part-time contract opportunities. This turns "competitors" into "partners."

- **Set Your Pay Scales:** Research local rates. Contract instructors typically earn between **$25 and $45 per hour**, while advanced certifications like ACLS or PALS often command **$35 to $55 per hour**.
- **Create an Instructor Portal:** Use a shared folder (Google Drive or Dropbox) where your team can access current lesson plans, digital student manuals, and your **Employee Handbook**.

Day 22: Create Local Partnerships

Local partnerships are the "force multipliers" of a safety training business. Instead of selling to one person at a time, partnerships allow you to sell to entire organizations. In the safety industry—where certifications are often legally required—positioning your business as the "preferred provider" for local institutions creates a recurring revenue stream that survives regardless of your marketing spend.

High-Value Strategic Partners

To maximize your reach across CPR, **driver safety**, and **food safety**, focus on these four pillars of the community:

- **Daycare Centers & Schools:** These are your most consistent clients. State laws usually require every staff member to be CPR/First Aid certified. Offer a "perpetual discount" for their staff in exchange for being their exclusive provider.
- **Health & Wellness Hubs:** Partner with local gyms, yoga studios, and senior centers. You can offer "Community Safety Days" where you provide free 15-minute AED demos to generate leads for full certification classes.

- **The "Restaurant Row":** Connect with local restaurant associations or supply stores. Since you offer **food safety** (ServSafe) and choking-relief training, you are a one-stop-shop for hospitality compliance.
- **Corporate Fleets & Insurance Agents:** Reach out to insurance brokers who handle commercial auto policies. They often encourage their clients to take **driver safety** courses to lower premiums. A referral from an insurance agent is a high-trust lead.

Structuring the "Win-Win"

A partnership only lasts if both sides benefit. When reaching out, move away from "selling" and toward "solving":

- **On-Site Convenience:** Offer to bring your **manikins** and equipment directly to their facility. This saves the partner money on employee travel time and logistics.
- **Co-Branded Marketing:** Offer to put the partner's logo on your website as a "Community Safety Partner." In return, ask to place your flyers in their breakroom or be mentioned in their monthly newsletter.

- **The "Host" Model:** If you don't have a permanent classroom, partner with a local community center or church. They provide the space for free or low cost, and you provide free training for their core staff.

Action Steps

- **Create a "Target 20" List:** Identify 20 local organizations (5 schools, 5 gyms, 5 restaurants, 5 corporate offices) that require safety training.
- **Develop a "Partner Perk" Sheet:** Create a simple one-page PDF outlining the benefits of a partnership: discounted rates, priority scheduling, and automated expiration reminders for their staff.
- **Offer a "Pilot" Session:** For large potential partners (like a school district), offer to train their leadership team at a reduced rate. This allows them to see your professional use of feedback **manikins** and high-quality instruction firsthand.
- **Automate the Relationship:** Use your booking system to create a unique "Partner Code." When their employees use that code, they get the discount, and you can easily track which partnerships are producing the most revenue.

DAY 23: CREATE BUSINESS CREDIT

Establishing business credit is about separating your personal financial identity from your company's. In the safety training industry, strong business credit allows you to finance high-ticket equipment—like a fleet of advanced, feedback-enabled **manikins** or a dedicated training vehicle—without risking your personal credit score. It also signals to large corporate clients and government agencies that your business is a stable, professional entity.

The Foundation of Business Credit

Unlike personal credit, which is tied to your Social Security Number, business credit is tied to your **Employer Identification Number (EIN)**. To build a "fundable" business, you must ensure your company looks like a separate entity in the eyes of lenders:

- **The "Lendability" Profile:** Ensure your business has a dedicated professional phone number and a physical address (avoid P.O. boxes). Lenders use automated bots to verify this data.
- **D-U-N-S Number:** Register for a free D-U-N-S number through **Dun & Bradstreet**.

This is the most widely used identifier for business credit. Without it, many vendors won't start a credit file for you.

- **Tracking Major Scores:** You should monitor three primary reports: the **Dun & Bradstreet Paydex Score** (focuses on payment speed), the **Experian Business Credit Profile** (looks at credit utilization and years in business), and the **Equifax Small Business** report.

The Business Credit Tier System

To build a high score without using your personal guarantee, you must climb through "Tiers." This prevents you from overextending before your business is ready.

- **Tier 1 (Vendor Credit):** These are companies that give you "Net-30" terms with almost no credit history.
  - *Examples:* **Quill, Uline, and Grainger.** Buy your sanitizing wipes, lung bags, or printer paper here.
- **Tier 2 (Store Credit):** Once you have 3–5 reporting lines from Tier 1, you can apply for store-branded cards.
  - *Examples:* **Amazon Business, Staples, and Home Depot.** Use these for tablets

used in training or furniture for your classroom.

- **Tier 3 (Fleet & Commercial Credit):** This tier is for established businesses with solid reporting history.
  - *Examples:* **WEX Fuel Cards, Shell Fleet, and Dell Business.** * *Advanced Financing:* At this stage, you can often secure vehicle financing under your business name through lenders like **Ally Business** or **Ford Pro**, and establish business lines of credit through institutions like **Navy Federal Credit Union** or local business-friendly banks.

Action Steps

- **Verify Your EIN & D-U-S:** Ensure you have your EIN from the IRS and apply for your D-U-N-S number today. It typically takes 7–14 days to process.
- **Open 3 Tier 1 Accounts:** Purchase small, necessary supplies for your next CPR or **food safety** class through vendors like Uline or Quill that report to the bureaus.
- **Pay Invoices Early:** For a perfect Paydex score, "on time" isn't enough. Paying 10–15 days early is what triggers the highest ratings.

- **Set Up Monitoring:** Use a service like **Nav** to monitor your Experian Business and Dun & Bradstreet scores in one place. This ensures no fraudulent accounts are opened and your vendors are reporting correctly.

DAY 24: CREATE PRINT MARKETING

In a digital world, physical marketing materials like brochures and flyers provide a "tangible" sense of trust. For a safety training business, print marketing serves as a constant reminder in breakrooms, community centers, and doctor's offices. When a business owner or a parent sees your professional flyer, it signals that you are a local, accessible expert ready to provide life-saving skills.

Designing for Impact

Your print materials should not just look good; they must be functional. Because you offer diverse services like CPR, **driver safety**, and **food safety**, your design needs to be organized:

- **The "Problem-Solution" Header:** Don't just put your logo at the top. Use a bold headline like *"Be the Difference in an Emergency"* or *"Is Your Kitchen Staff Fully Compliant?"*
- **The QR Code Shortcut:** Every piece of paper you print should have a large, scannable QR code that leads directly to your **booking page**. This removes the friction of a customer having to type in a URL.

- **High-Resolution Equipment Shots:** Use those high-quality photos of your **manikins** and AED trainers from Day 16. Seeing modern equipment on a brochure reassures corporate clients that they aren't getting "outdated" training.
- **The "Social Proof" Snippet:** Include a one-sentence testimonial from a local local business or healthcare professional.

Strategic Distribution: Where Your Clients Are

Don't just leave a stack of flyers on a random coffee shop table. Target locations where your specific audience congregates:

- **For CPR & First Aid:** Pediatrician offices, local gyms, community centers, and places of worship.
- **For Driver Safety:** Local insurance agencies (who can offer discounts for your course) and high school guidance offices.
- **For Food Safety:** Restaurant supply stores, commercial kitchens, and local health department waiting rooms.

Choosing the Right Print Partner

You need a balance between cost and quality. For safety training, "premium" feel matters.

- **Short Runs (Flyers/Posters):** Use local shops or services like **Canva Print** or **FedEx Office** for quick turnarounds.
- **Bulk Runs (Brochures/Booklets):** Use online commercial printers like **Vistaprint** or **GotPrint** to get a lower price per unit.
- **Paper Stock:** Opt for a "matte" or "glossy" finish on a heavier cardstock. A thin, flimsy flyer suggests a "budget" operation; a sturdy brochure suggests a professional institution.

Action Steps

- **Create Your "Brand Toolkit":** Use a tool like **Canva** to design one standard flyer and one tri-fold brochure. Ensure your colors match your website for brand consistency.
- **Order a "Sample Pack":** Before ordering 500 brochures, order a small batch of 25 to check for typos and ensure the QR code scans correctly.
- **Execute the "Target 10" Drop:** Identify the top 10 locations in your city where your target audience spends time. Spend one afternoon

personally delivering a stack of 20 brochures
to each, introducing yourself to the manager.

- **Track Your Results:** Use a specific "tracking
  link" or a unique coupon code (e.g., "FLYER10")
  on your print materials so you know exactly
  which location is sending you the most
  students.

Day 25: Create An Advertising Strategy

A successful advertising strategy isn't just about spending money; it's about appearing where people are already looking for safety. By 2026, the most effective marketing for safety businesses blends **high-intent digital search** with **local community visibility**. Whether you are targeting a parent looking for "infant CPR" or a trucking fleet manager needing "driver safety" compliance, your strategy must prove you are the most reliable expert in their area.

Digital Strategy: Capturing High-Intent Leads

Most people search for safety training only when they have an immediate need (a job requirement, a new baby, or a license renewal). Your ads should meet them at that moment of need.

- **Google Search Ads (PPC):** This is often the highest ROI channel. Bid on "long-tail" keywords like *"BLS certification for nurses [City Name]"* or *"ServSafe manager exam [City Name]."* These users are ready to buy **now**.

- **Local Services Ads (LSAs):** If available in your region, these "Google Guaranteed" ads appear at the very top of search results. They focus on local trust and show your 5-star rating and "Verified" status.
- **Retargeting Ads:** Use a tracking pixel on your website. If someone visits your **driver safety** page but doesn't book, show them a helpful ad on Facebook or Instagram a day later with a student testimonial to nudge them back.

Content That Resonates

In safety training, your "creative" should focus on **confidence** and **consequence**. Use the "Before vs. After" psychology:

- **The "Before":** Highlight the anxiety of not knowing what to do in a crisis (e.g., "Would you know what to do if your driver hit a patch of ice?").
- **The "After":** Show the confidence of a trained professional using high-tech **manikins** or simulators.
- **Visual Trust:** Your ads should feature your actual kit—clean **manikins**, modern AED trainers, and professional certificates—to distance yourself from "basement instructors."

Traditional & Offline "Boosters"

While digital is king, local safety is still a "face-to-face" business:

- **The "Truck Magnet" Strategy:** If you have a training vehicle, ensure it is professionally wrapped with your services: *CPR | Driver Safety | Food Safety.* It serves as a mobile billboard every time you drive to a client site.
- **Sponsorships:** Sponsor a local youth sports league. You can provide the coaches with free CPR training in exchange for your logo on the field or in the parent newsletter.

Action Steps

- **Set a "Test Budget":** Start with **$5 to $10 per day** on Google Search Ads. Focus on your most profitable class first (usually corporate group training).
- **Audit Your Ad Copy:** Ensure every ad has a clear Call to Action (CTA). Instead of "We teach CPR," use *"Get Certified Today – Same Day eCards!"*
- **Set Up Conversion Tracking:** Ensure your Google Ads account is linked to your booking software. You need to know exactly which ad

led to a paid student so you can scale what works.

- **Claim Your "Map Pack":** Check your Google Business Profile (from Day 18) to ensure your "Ads" lead to a profile full of recent, high-quality photos of your training kit.

DAY 26: DOING BUSINESS WITH THE GOVERNMENT

Government contracts—local, state, and federal—are the "holy grail" of safety training. Agencies like police departments, park services, and municipal offices have massive staff counts that require recurring certifications. Unlike individual students, a government contract provides a steady, multi-year revenue stream that is often "recession-proof."

Getting "Government Ready"

Before you can bid on a contract, you must prove that your business is a legitimate, compliant entity. Government agencies do not "just buy"; they follow strict procurement protocols.

- **Register with SAM.gov:** The **System for Award Management (SAM)** is the primary database of vendors doing business with the federal government. You must register here to be eligible for federal contracts.
- **Get Your UEI:** The **Unique Entity ID (UEI)** has replaced the D-U-N-S number for federal

contracting. You will receive this during your SAM registration.

- **Identify Your NAICS Codes:** These are numerical codes used to classify your business. For safety training, you will likely use:
  - **611699:** All Other Miscellaneous Schools and Instruction
  - **611430:** Professional and Management Development Training
- **CAGE Code:** Once you register in SAM, you will be assigned a **Commercial and Government Entity (CAGE)** code, which is required for payments and security clearances.

Finding Opportunities: Where to Look

You don't have to wait for a "Request for Proposal" (RFP) to land in your lap. You can proactively find "Set-Aside" contracts reserved for small businesses:

- **Local Municipalities:** Check the "Procurement" or "Purchasing" tab on your city and county websites. They often need CPR for lifeguards and **driver safety** for public works employees.
- **School Districts:** Every public school needs CPR/First Aid for coaches and teachers.

- **State Contracts:** Most states have a central portal (e.g., "eVA" in Virginia or "Cal eProcure" in California) where you can register as a vendor.

Strategic Advantage: Small Business Designations

The government has goals to award a percentage of contracts to specific groups. If you qualify for any of the following, your chances of winning a bid increase significantly:

- **Woman-Owned Small Business (WOSB)**
- **Service-Disabled Veteran-Owned Small Business (SDVOSB)**
- **8(a) Business Development Program** (for socially and economically disadvantaged individuals)
- **HUBZone** (businesses located in historically underutilized business zones)

Action Steps

- **Register for your SAM.gov account:** This is a detailed process—set aside 2–3 hours to complete it accurately.
- **Build a "Capability Statement":** This is a one-page "resume" for your business. It

should highlight your certifications, your use of feedback-enabled **manikins**, and your ability to scale for large groups.

- **Reach out to your local SBDC:** The **Small Business Development Center** or **PTAC** (Procurement Technical Assistance Center) offers free counseling to help you navigate the government bidding process.
- **Start Small with "Micro-Purchases":** Federal agencies can often spend up to $10,000 without a formal bidding process. Call local offices (VA hospitals, military bases, forest service) and offer your services for small staff groups to get your foot in the door.

Day 27: Build Your Client Base With Email Marketing

In the safety industry, email marketing is your primary tool for **automated retention**. Because CPR, **food safety**, and **driver safety** certifications expire every 1 to 2 years, your email list is essentially a list of guaranteed future sales. By staying in your clients' inboxes, you ensure they come back to *you* rather than searching Google for a competitor when their card is about to expire.

The "Lifecycle" Email Strategy

Don't just send random updates; move your clients through a deliberate journey:

- **The Welcome Sequence:** When someone signs up for your newsletter or a class, send an immediate "Welcome" email. Include a free "Emergency Preparedness Checklist" or a "Safety Myth-Busters" PDF to establish your authority.
- **The Educational "Drip":** Send monthly tips that add value. For example, "3 Common Mistakes People Make During the Heimlich Maneuver"

or "How to Check Your Fleet's Tire Tread in 10 Seconds."

- **The "Expiration" Countdown:** This is your most profitable email. Set up automated reminders starting **60 days** before a student's certification expires. Send follow-ups at 30 days and 14 days.
- **The Corporate "Nurture":** Send quarterly compliance updates to your B2B contacts (HR managers and restaurant owners). Mention new state regulations or upgrades in your **manikin** technology to show you are a high-end provider.

Designing for Trust and Action

Safety emails should be clean, professional, and easy to read on a mobile device.

- **Subject Lines that Matter:** Avoid "Salesy" language. Use clear headers like *"Action Required: Your CPR Certification Expires in 30 Days"* or *"Safety Alert: Is your kitchen ready for a surprise inspection?"*
- **Clear Call-to-Action (CTA):** Every email should have one big, obvious button that says **"Renew My Certification"** or **"Book a Private Group Class."**

- **Visual Proof:** Include a photo of your modern training kit or a short video of a student successfully using a feedback **manikin.** This reminds them of the high quality they can expect.

Choosing Your "Email Engine"

You need a platform that allows for **segmentation** (grouping people by class type) and **automation.**

- **Mailchimp / Constant Contact:** Great for beginners with easy "drag and drop" templates.
- **Klaviyo / ActiveCampaign:** Better for advanced automation and deep integration with your booking software.
- **Specialized CRM:** If your booking software has built-in email tools, use them first to keep your data in one place.

Action Steps

- **Import Your Roster:** Gather every email address from past classes and upload them into your chosen platform (ensure you have permission to email them).

- **Create Your "Renewal" Automation:** Build a simple 3-email sequence that triggers automatically based on a student's "certification date."
- **Design a "Lead Magnet":** Create a simple PDF (e.g., "The Top 5 Items Every Workplace First Aid Kit Needs") to offer on your website in exchange for an email address.
- **Segment Your List:** Create tags for "CPR Students," "Food Safety Managers," and "Fleet Owners." This ensures you don't send a driver safety tip to a nurse who only needs BLS.

Day 28: Find New CPR And Safety Training Clients Through Networking

In the safety industry, networking isn't just about "selling"—it's about becoming a trusted advisor in the community. People buy safety training from people they know and trust. By positioning yourself as the go-to expert for CPR, **driver safety**, and **food safety**, you turn "cold" leads into "warm" referrals.

Strategic Networking: Where to Show Up

To find high-value clients, you must go where decision-makers and high-risk groups congregate. Focus on these three specific circles:

- **Chambers of Commerce & BNI:** These groups are filled with local business owners who have employees to certify. Use these meetings to offer "Safety Audits" rather than just classes.
- **Industry-Specific Associations:** * **Healthcare:** Join local nursing associations or dental societies.

- ○ **Hospitality:** Attend restaurant association meetups (perfect for **food safety**).
- ○ **Logistics:** Join transportation or fleet manager forums (ideal for **driver safety**).
- **Safety & HR Conferences:** Human Resource managers are your primary "gatekeepers" for corporate contracts. Attending HR-focused events allows you to solve their "compliance headache" directly.

The "Expert" Elevator Pitch

When someone asks what you do, don't just say, "I teach CPR." Use a pitch that highlights your unique value and modern technology:

> *"I help local businesses stay compliant and save lives by providing high-tech safety training. We use feedback-enabled manikins that guarantee your staff actually knows what to do in a crisis, rather than just watching a video."*

Digital Networking & Strategic Follow-Up

Meeting someone is only 10% of the work; the other 90% is the follow-up.

- **LinkedIn Connectivity:** After meeting someone at an event, send a personalized LinkedIn invite within 24 hours. Mention a specific detail from your conversation.
- **The "Value-Add" Follow-Up:** Instead of asking for a sale, send a helpful resource. *"Hi [Name], it was great meeting you at the Chamber event. I thought you might find this 'Office Safety Checklist' useful for your team."*
- **Host a "Lunch & Learn":** Invite 3–5 local business owners to a free 30-minute demonstration of your AED trainers and **manikins**. It's a low-pressure way to show off your expertise.

Action Steps

- **Join One Local Group This Week:** Find a local BNI chapter or Chamber of Commerce and register as a guest for their next meeting.
- **Update Your LinkedIn Profile:** Ensure your headline clearly states your services: *CPR, Driver Safety, and Food Safety Training for [City/Region].*
- **Prepare Your "Leave-Behinds":** Ensure you have high-quality business cards or the print brochures we designed on Day 24 ready to hand out.

- **The "Double-Sided" Referral:** Reach out to a past client and offer them a "referral credit." If they introduce you to another business owner who books a class, give them a discount on their next re-certification.

Day 29: Spread the Word to Your Local Community

Local awareness is the lifeblood of a safety training business. While digital ads reach people *searching* for you, community outreach reaches people who *need* you but haven't looked yet. By becoming a visible fixture in your town, you move from being a "vendor" to a "community safety partner."

Strategic Community Presence

Focus on high-visibility opportunities where you can demonstrate your expertise in CPR, **driver safety**, and **food safety** through hands-on interaction:

- **Public Safety Demonstrations:** Don't just set up a booth; set up a **manikin station.** Offer "2-Minute CPR Lessons" at farmers' markets, street fairs, or high school football games. People who wouldn't normally sign up for a

4-hour class will stop for a quick demo—and that's when you hand them your brochure.

- **School & Youth Group Workshops:** Reach out to PTA groups and scout troops. Offer to do a "First Aid for Kids" session. While the kids learn, you are building trust with the parents (your primary customers).
- **Safety "Pop-Ups" at Local Businesses:** Partner with a local hardware store or pharmacy to host a "Safety Saturday." You provide free AED demos, and they provide the space. It's a win-win that drives foot traffic for both of you.

Leveraging Hyper-Local Digital Channels

Beyond traditional social media, use platforms specifically designed for neighborhoods:

- **Nextdoor:** Join Nextdoor as a "Local Business." Share helpful safety tips (e.g., "How to prevent choking during holiday meals") rather than just ads. People on Nextdoor value neighbors helping neighbors.
- **Local Facebook Groups:** Participate in "Town Square" or "Moms and Dads of [City]" groups. When someone asks for a recommendation

for a CPR class, your name should be the one that everyone mentions.

- **Patch & Local News:** Send a press release to your local digital newspaper when you launch a new initiative, like a "Scholarship Program" for low-income residents to get certified.

The "Demonstration" Advantage

In the safety industry, seeing is believing. Use your modern equipment as a marketing tool:

- **Visual Trust:** When you are out in the community, use your most advanced **manikins**. The visual of a high-tech feedback monitor catching someone's attention is worth a thousand flyers.
- **Interactive Contests:** Host a "Who can get the best compression score?" contest using your feedback devices. Give the winner a small prize or a discount code for a full certification.

Action Steps

- **Book One Community Event:** Look at your city's events calendar for the next 3 months. Contact the organizer of a health fair or community market today to secure a booth.

- **The "Safety Starter" Pack:** Create a simple 1-page "Local Emergency Contact List" branded with your logo. Distribute these to local daycare centers to post on their fridges.
- **Nextdoor Business Profile:** Claim your business page on Nextdoor and ask three past students from your neighborhood to leave a recommendation.
- **Offer a Free "Hands-Only" Session:** Reach out to a local library or senior center and offer to do a free 30-minute non-certification demo. It's the perfect way to build a mailing list for your paid classes.

Day 30: Create an Unforgettable Launch Event for your CPR and Safety Training Business

The launch event is more than just a "grand opening"—it is a live demonstration of your expertise. For a safety training business, this is your chance to prove that learning life-saving skills doesn't have to be intimidating or dry. By showcasing your modern **manikins**, your professional instructors, and your diverse curriculum (CPR, **driver safety**, and **food safety**), you turn curious neighbors into lifelong clients.

Designing an Interactive "Safety Showcase"

A great launch event should be hands-on. Instead of a long speech, create "Safety Stations" where guests can rotate through different skills:

- **The Compression Challenge:** Use your feedback-enabled **manikins** to run a "Top Scorer" contest. Guests can see their real-time depth and rate on a screen. It's fun, competitive, and proves the value of your technology.

- **The Choking Rescue Station:** Use a choking vest or trainer to show guests how to perform the Heimlich maneuver correctly. This is a high-impact, emotional skill that everyone wants to know.
- **The AED Demo:** Many people are afraid of AEDs. Set up a trainer unit and let guests hear the voice prompts. Once they realize how easy it is to use, their confidence in your training will skyrocket.
- **Driver & Food Safety Corner:** Have a tablet set up with a "Safety Quiz" for **driver safety** or a "Spot the Hazard" game for **food safety**. Offer a small prize, like a branded keychain or a first-aid kit, for participation.

Strategic Logistics

- **The Venue:** If you have a physical classroom, host it there! If you are a mobile business, partner with a local community center, gym, or even a popular local cafe to host a "Safety Social."
- **The "VIP" Invite List:** Invite local HR managers, daycare directors, and restaurant owners. Give them a "VIP Safety Pack" that includes your pricing model and a special "Grand Opening" discount for their first group booking.

- **Food & Atmosphere:** Keep it light. Offer "Healthy Heart" snacks or partner with a local catering client to provide refreshments (a great way to cross-promote with a **food safety** partner).

Marketing the Launch

- **Social Media Countdown:** Use the 7 days leading up to the event to "tease" your equipment. Post a video of your **manikins** being unboxed or your instructors prepping the space.
- **Local Media:** Send a short press release to your local newspaper or radio station. "New Local Business Aims to Heart-Start the Community" is a great hook.
- **Eventbrite / Facebook Events:** Create a digital RSVP system so you can collect email addresses (for your Day 27 Email Strategy!) before the event even starts.

Action Steps

- **Set Your Date:** Choose a Saturday morning or a weekday evening when local business owners and parents are most likely to be available.

- **Secure Your "Door Prizes":** Ask local partners (gyms, healthy restaurants) to donate items for a raffle. This creates a "community feel" and encourages people to stay until the end.
- **The "Book-On-Site" Special:** Offer a 20% discount for anyone who registers for a class during the launch event. Have a tablet ready at the door for immediate sign-ups.
- **Document the Day:** Hire a photographer or ask a friend to take high-quality photos and videos. This "Launch Content" will fuel your social media and website for months to come.

About The Author

Timeka Mapp is a happy, healthy, successful, and prosperous visionary who enjoys living life to the fullest. Born in **Atlanta, Georgia**, she began her journey as a writer at an early age. When she is not writing, she can often be found wandering through nature on a hike or journaling at a local coffee shop.

Timeka is the author of **"The Today Goal"** and other impactful books designed to inspire and empower her readers. Through her work, she combines her visionary outlook with practical steps to help others achieve their own versions of success and prosperity.

Find out more at: https://amazon.com/author/timeka

www.ingramcontent.com/pod-product-compliance
Lightning Source LLC
Chambersburg PA
CBHW071159200326
41519CB00018B/5287